10 HACKS FOR Working IN NAIJA

'The untold secrets for thriving in the work place in Nigeria'

I0504935

With 2
Bonus
Chapters!

10 HACKS FOR Working IN NAIJA

'The untold secrets for thriving in the work place in Nigeria'

Copyright

© 2019 by Temitope George

The right of Temitope George to be identified as the author and publisher of this work has been asserted by her in accordance with copyright laws.

Cover Design by: 'Lekan Adesanya

Printed by: Anesis Global Concepts Limited

Acknowledgments

Be quick to learn, after you have learnt, teach.

Acknowledgments

IN NAIJA' *by Temitope George*

"A truly easy to read and good reference guide, reflecting factual experiences that often occur in the workplace. Temitope has indeed called out the "Elephant in the Room" with her "HACKS." A must read especially for a JJC to the corporate world."

Odiri Erewa-Meggison, Head of   Marketing Legal, British American Tobacco, Indonesia

"My best hacks from the book are Hack 11 (Past glory doesn't last), Hack 5 (Confidence is key), and Hack 10 (Be quick to learn, after you have learnt, teach). To learn from the experience of others is priceless and certainly a lot cheaper than learning from own. On this basis, the book is a must read. With this said, there is a hack not fully highlighted in the book but demonstrated by the author and that is the 'go-getter attitude'. With bags of energy and a result driven orientation, Temitope from writing this book, demonstrates what is perhaps most important for career growth; The can do, go-getter mentality all employers are looking for…Temitope simply thinks it and goes ahead to do it."

Tawa Bolarin, Chief Executive Officer,GBAMNigeriaLimited.

"A very insightful and practical guide to workplace success. I recommend Temitope's Hacks to anyone starting out in their career. I certainly hope all our employees read this book. Well done TG" –
Michael A. Owolabi, MD /CEO Ilbagno Nigeria Ltd.

Acknowledgments

"I really enjoyed reading Hacks for Working in Naija. I found hack 2 so apt yet so funny; don't just look the part, smell the part. Hack 3 is so key, as a lot of us fail to make ourselves visible and speak up when required. Temitope captures these lessons so well. She ends beautifully with hack 12; keeping a trail of certain conversations. This is one lesson I have to remind myself to do. In a world with very interesting individuals it is essential to err on the side of caution always."

Folaseto Akin-Olugbade, Invesment Professional, Actis

"From an intern starting her first job to a seasoned worker looking to learn new tricks to move up the corporate ladder, Temitope's comprehensively compiled hacks are guaranteed to aid in navigating the Nigerian workplace. By giving real life examples, Temitope effectively and succinctly sums up the unique challenges Nigerians face in the workplace and the best way to tackle the various issues that often arise."

Jumoke Salami, Former Regional Vendor Management Lead for Middle East and Africa at Nielsen.

"10 hacks for working in Naija is the absolute eye-opener for anyone looking to work in the private sector either as an employee or employer. It is really insightful, value-packed and simple to read. The best part of it is how 'snackable' and easily digestible each chapter is. I just wanted to read chapters 1-3 and read the rest later. Before I knew it, I read the whole book. I'm not that patient when it comes to reading books but I found myself flipping back to back for more. The case studies and scenarios used as examples make the book more fun to read. I surely recommend this to everyone serious about taking the leap in his or her career. Whether you are in school, or out of school or looking to get employed or to employ people, this is your best resource. A must read!!!"

Bamidele Olamilekan (KingPexxie) Legal practitioner, Brand builder.

10 HACKS FOR Working IN NAIJA

'The untold secrets for thriving in the work place in Nigeria'

"Temitope has found a concise and easy way to capture the essence of what millennials require to blend into the Nigerian corporate workspace and ultimately thrive. This book encapsulates important navigation tools that will help millennials settle, fit in and better understand bosses and colleagues. She captures the hacks in an easy to read and humorous way, using unique Nigerian language and nuances with clear and memorable takeaways after each hack. I definitely recommend this as a must read for young folks looking to excel in the Nigerian corporate workspace."

Dr. Femi Johnson, MD/CEO Homebase Mortgage Bank, past president of Mortgage Banking Association of Nigeria.

"The Nigerian workplace can be like a minefield, and those who successfully navigate it do so, not by accident, but by being smart and strategic. The question is how? And the answer is right here: Temitope has written a fantastic guidebook for those who desire to not just survive but thrive at work. It's an incredibly engaging and practical book that you will find useful, whether you're just starting out in your career or you're already a workplace veteran. The workplace hacks in the book are masterfully brought to life through relatable real life illustrations. From cultivating the right attitude to handling difficult people, this book truly holds the secrets of success for a truly fulfilling workplace experience."

Ogochukwu Nwokedi Head, Voyage Management & Agency, Nigeria LNG Ltd.

Acknowledgments

I am thankful to the greatest storyteller, who I credit for the inspiration to share truths and real life experiences through stories. Dear Lord, thank you.

I have a number of bosses to thank for the exposure and many hacks they were giving me unknowingly, but I will mention a few of them.

First, I would like to thank Ms. Ida Denise Drameh, of Macaulay QC & Drameh for showing me the importance of a good name. Her name opened doors for me far away from the shores of Gambia.

Mr. Gbenga Oyebode of Aluko & Oyebode for the many hacks on the go and your very witty quotes – "you don't always get what you deserve, you may get what you work for but you always get what's coming to you." Thank you, GO.

Mr. Ayo Gbeleyi, the first Director-General of the first Lagos State Public Private Partnership Office and former Commissioner of Finance, Lagos State. Thank you for keeping me on my toes and making me go over that report just one more time, which eventually saved me from your famous 'redlines.'

Mrs. Abimbola Fashola aka Iyar, the Chairperson and Founder, Leadership, Empowerment & Resource Network (L.E.A.R.N), thank you for trusting me to lead your 'passion project' and thereby helping me discover a passion for working with teens.

My husband Obafemi aka bestie, thank you for being my greatest cheerleader. Your belied that I can do absolutely anything I put my

Acknowledgments

mind to, keeps pushing me to keep doing all that God places in my heart to do and more. Tito, Teni and Oba, my three musketeers, thank you for allowing me to still 'do me' while being your mum.

Mum and Dad, thank you for giving me the leverage to be who I am today.

Ogo Nwokedi, thank you for encouraging me to tell these stories and giving valuable feedback.

And finally, to my followers on Instagram: @thetemitopegeorge who take out time to watch my videos and leave comments and direct messages, I hope I have done justice to the experiences you shared with me. Please keep them coming.

Thank you.

Contents

FOREWORD

The 10 Hacks for Working in Naija delivers interesting accounts and perspectives on workplace hazards within the Nigerian context. This book is an excellent resource to employees, workers, supervisors, and managers who want to build a career for themselves in the African state environment. While the hacks cited may seem like everyday workplace conditions, the lessons embedded in their contents will be useful to the reader. The best part is that the 10 hacks are backed with real-life scenarios and cases.

The reader is taken on a journey through the Nigerian work environment and receives first-hand accounts from experienced employees and professionals who have attained career excellence in various pursuits while they learned the lessons the hard way – through personal experiences, some of which were unpleasant. The tone of the book reflects a learned appreciation for shared experiences and impact in respect to workplace success and failure as illustrated by Maya Angelou's quote, "When you learn, teach. When you get, give."

The author, Temitope George is a British Trained Barrister (of Gray's Inn) and a Legal Practitioner of the Supreme Court of Nigeria with over 16 years' experience that cuts across all levels in the private and public sector. In addition to acting as a facilitator and career coach for such organizations as LEAP Africa School-to-Work Programme and several undergraduates at various tertiary institutions, she has also facilitated career-building programmes for FifthGear Consulting marketplace readiness programme with the National Youth Service Corps of Nigeria. Her years of experience in training others on workplace readiness, professional etiquette, and executive presence on numerous platforms establish her in a strategic position to gather and assemble key nuggets on how employees can become proactive in their relations at work.

10 Hacks for Working in Naija is a priced jewel to any Naija working professional looking to scale up the ladder amidst all odds. I strongly recommend it to that employee who wants to overcome several workplace hazards. The application of the principles in the book will help you become an expert market place professional.

Niyi Adesanya,
Management Consultant,
CEO, Fifthgearplus Consulting

INTRODUCTION

Segun started his first job having graduated with First Class in Engineering from the University of Ibadan. He almost lost his job in the first week because he sent correspondence to the wrong recipient, a mistake that could have been avoided if he knew of *Hack 6*.

Ada was successful in a graduate placement after relocating back to Nigeria, following her degree at the University of Essex. Six (6) months on, she is thinking of quitting her job and going back to England because in spite of working long and late hours, her supervisors say they don't see what she is doing. Ada didn't know the importance of *Hack 3*, especially when working in a Nigerian environment.

The aim of this book is to prepare people like Ada and Segun to kick off their career in a unique workplace culture like Nigeria.

These lessons from my boss (referred to here as hacks) are based on real life experiences of people who have attained career excellence in various pursuits. The names are however fictitious to protect the details of their organisations. The employees mentioned learnt the lessons the hard way – through personal experiences, some of which were unpleasant. Experience is the best teacher, they say, but those experiences don't have to be yours!

With these hacks you will not only survive in the work place, you will thrive.

She continued to apply the same principle of seeking relevance by working hard, without focusing on immediate gratification.

Hack 1

TO WORK IS A PRIVILEGE. WORK HARD.

Do yourself a favour and work hard at anything and everything you are assigned. Remember that having work to do is a privilege not a right!

Anike had just finished her Masters in Business Administration (MBA) in the United Kingdom (UK) and knew she needed tangible work experience before going back to Nigeria. Since she did not have UK work experience, she settled for a call centre agent role.

Anike had two job opportunities for call centre agents. One was a start-up and the other was an already established company. Anike chose the start-up because she felt the start-up would give her an expanded opportunity to learn more about the industry and to grow.

Based on her contributions during the mandatory training for new call centre agents, she was immediately approached by the call centre manager to take on a new role. The role was back office support for the call center. This presented an opportunity to learn about the operational aspect of the business and to interface with Head Quarters (HQ) for decision support. Although it was more work, the salary was the same as a call centre agent and the job grade was still entry level. Nevertheless, Anike was excited at this opportunity because for her, it gave her a chance to do more work and learn more.

Four months into the back office job, a Senior Director in HQ approached her to look into a business problem. Anike finally had her first opportunity to blend the analytical skills gained in business

Hack 1

school, with the knowledge of the telecoms operation she had been exposed to over the past four months. She spent after working hours and several nights, analyzing data, working hard to solve the business problem, resulting in the production of a comprehensive business plan, presented to the HQ Senior Director.

Anike was just glad to have an opportunity to increase her relevance at her workplace, without expecting any reward. The reward that came from the business plan presentation was one that Anike could never have imagined. Two weeks later, the Senior Director asked her to apply for a role as Product Manager. Incidentally, the company had decided to disengage the previous role holder. One thing was clear to the Senior Director, Anike was needed in HQ to help grow the new business. So, five months after taking a less than desired role as a call centre agent, Anike became a Product Manager. This time, she had a full job grade change and more than 100% increase in salary.

Anike's work in the UK created an opportunity for her to move back to Nigeria in the same industry and she continued to apply the same principle of seeking relevance by working hard, without focusing on immediate gratification. After more than a decade in the Telecoms industry where she rose to the position of a Director, heading a business division, she is now the Chief Executive Officer (CEO) of a startup which, for her, presents an exciting opportunity to learn and gain relevance in an entirely new industry.

Takeaways:

Hack 1

TO WORK IS A PRIVILEGE. WORK HARD.

1. Always take on more than you can handle. Stretch yourself. The assignments she took on were learning opportunities for her and taught her all she knew in her workplace and other roles she took on.

2. Grabbing opportunities to learn more even without immediate remuneration was her focus.

    Anike wasn't like many of her classmates who were after instant gratification, wanting to do the barest minimum and be paid handsomely for it. Of course she wanted money but she soon realized that once you are hardworking and willing to do more than you are paid to, money would follow. It always does.

3. Success at work lies in not saying 'No' to whatever work is thrown at you. Ask someone, read up, burn the midnight oil, your reward will come and like Anike, it will be exponential, if you keep working hard.

4. It is important to note that everyone at the workplace is bargaining for more! More money, more recognition, but what gives you an edge is if you do more, learn more and take on more than you are paid to. Working hard and taking on more tasks is your competitive edge.

Hack 1
TO WORK IS A PRIVILEGE. WORK HARD.

Your good looking CV has given you a foot in the door but to keep you there, you must also look the part and dare I say, smell the part too.

Hack 2
Don't just look the part, smell the part.

It goes without saying that when applying for a job your Curriculum Vitae (CV) must look good. By looking good I am not saying it should be full of false embellishments. I simply mean, it is important to put your best foot forward, but in so doing, you must be able to substantiate your accomplishments. It pays to actually get a professional to review your CV, to ensure it is the best representation of you. Don't forget to include all those little things that make you look good such as how you volunteered to teach once a week in a high school while you were in University or being a Lector at church - unique details that are peculiar to you.

Your good-looking CV has given you a foot in the door but to keep you there, you must also look the part and dare I say, smell the part too. Some organisations are very particular about the way their employees look that they give them clothing allowance and prescribe colours that they should wear. This is not unusual if you are in the Marketing department of a bank, for example. However, even where you do not receive a dress allowance, you will do well to not only look your best but smell good too.

Farouk, a good looking guy with a great CV and numerous accolades in tow, was not retained after his National Youth Service

Hack 2

Don't just look the part, smell the part.

Corps (NYSC) simply because whenever he went to a particular floor in the organisation which housed the key decision makers, they would smile and nod and start shutting their doors. This good-looking guy had a pervasive odour and no one in the organisation had the nerve to tell him. He was indisputably one of the smartest guys in the organisation, and it came as a rude shock to many that he wasn't retained after NYSC, but the unspoken reason became clear when he left. He didn't smell good.

Body Odour and **Mouth Odour** are hazardous to your career! Invest in your personal hygiene.

Takeaways:

1. Due to the tropical nature of the Nigerian weather, using a deodorant is not optional. For females, using the stronger male deodorant may be your best option.

2. Invest in good oral hygiene – brushing properly, flossing and the use of mouthwash when necessary, especially when you're fasting.

3. It goes without saying that when you smell good, you feel good and should also look good too. Your total appearance matters.

Hack 2

Don't just look the part, smell the part.

4. Seek medical attention in case of chronic body, mouth or other pervasive odour.

The work place is not a place where you do good deeds in secret. No way! Your good works, indeed any type of work must be done in the full glare of everyone.

Hack 3
Be visible.

Chioma is extroverted, so more often than not, you see or hear her coming, however when it comes to work, she likes to drill down quietly and focus on what she needs to get done, and just do it. In essence, as jovial and loud as she can be in informal situations, she just didn't make so much noise about her work. She was a firm believer in just getting on with it, until she had the following conversation with her boss.

Boss: Hey, how is it going?

Chioma: Very well, Sir.

Boss: Hmm, I don't see you or hear your voice much?

Chioma: Sir, you know I am hardworking and I am too busy upstairs, getting my work done.

Boss: That's not enough.

Chioma: (*in shock*) Sir, you see my reports, you know I am doing my work.

Boss: I know, but it's not enough; everyone else needs to know that too!

Hack 3

Be visible.

Then her boss proceeded to tell her about a colleague in the same office. At that office, there was only one colour printer at the time, and a lot of the time there were a lot of documents on the queue to be printed.

The practice was that if anyone wanted to print on letter headed paper, the person would have to shout out *'Printing!'* to alert others that they needed to print, to prevent them printing on letter headed paper. Letter headed paper suggested sending out a letter or opinion to a client. Essentially, it suggested that the person was working. This colleague would shout 'printing!' and walk briskly to the central printer, which was about 10 feet away from him.

Her boss continued, 'you see, with Mr. X, there is no doubt that he is working' to which she reluctantly agreed. Mr. X wasn't the most liked guy at work. In fact, he could be quite irritating most times, however what no one could argue with, was the fact that he was always shouting 'Printing', which translated to 'Working'. When his contemporaries were overlooked for a promotion, he certainly wasn't!

She walked away from her boss, wondering how he could be praising 'eye service'. "Why do I need to let everyone see that I am working? Can't I just do my work in peace?" And what she couldn't understand at the time was that, unfortunately you couldn't. Your colleagues and supervisors need to see that you are working. The work place is not a place where you do good deeds in secret. No way! Your good works, indeed any type of work must be done in the full glare of everyone. No *'right hand covering what the left hand is doing'* at the Nigerian workplace, you must *'loud it'* (make it obvious). It is important to note however that, while it is not sufficient to be working hard quietly, you also cannot be *'forming*

Hack 3

Be visible.

busy' (pretending you're working) when you're not, as sooner or later you will be exposed. If you're running around acting like you're busy but your output at work doesn't match up, this will also become apparent to your boss and colleagues, eventually. So, work hard and let it show that you're working hard, but don't make a show of being hardworking when you're hardly working, as that will also be clear to all.

Being visible at the work place is not optional; it is critical to your career success.

Takeaways:

1. Make sure to get your work done, but ensure your colleagues, supervisors, and key decision makers know and see you getting it done too.

Hack 3
Be visible.

2. Ensure that you are actually doing the work, and do not make a show of working when you are not as that would also be visible to all, eventually.

3. Seek out the quality traits that are rewarded at your company, and make sure you embody them.

4. If in doubt, look at how other 'star' employees are getting ahead, and copy their style while incorporating your personal touch.

Hack 4

Know your work.

Knowing your work, seems a very obvious work place hack doesn't it? After all, if you don't know your work, why are you even there? Understanding the details of your work, the nitty gritty including the footnotes, and being prepared to talk about them, is key. Furthermore, as you advance in your career you should not only constantly take stock of your daily tasks but achievements, as well.

As a new employee, Bisi was so excited to be working in the law firm of her dreams. One day as she returned from her court appearance with a Senior Associate in the law firm, she bumped into the Managing Partner in the elevator. The Managing Partner said, "Bisi, how are you and where are you coming from?"

"Sir, I am coming from court," Bisi said with excitement. "You know I love litigation," she gushed.

'What was the claim?' Bisi's boss asked.

Bisi was ill-prepared for the question and started stuttering. The elevator doors opened just in time, but not before her boss shook his head and said, 'you like court so much but you can't remember what you went for?'

Bisi of course knew what the claim and cause of action were, but at the time she wasn't expecting the questions and that made her look like she didn't know her work. What happened to Bisi may

Hack 4

Know your work.

sound familiar right? Bisi learnt a valuable lesson that day, and as she has risen in the ranks in her career, whenever she handles a file on her job she scans through it every time in readiness to be asked a question in respect of it. More often than not she is over-prepared for an elevator pitch with the boss, and indeed with anyone and has never been caught unawares since then.

I am sure you can relate to at least one occasion where you felt you didn't perform as well as you should have or you were asked a question and mumbled through an answer, but a moment later you were able to answer it perfectly.

The trick is to anticipate scenarios and daily take stock of your activities at work. If you are taking stock, writing things down and internalizing them daily, you won't forget when you are required to talk about your work. You also need to prepare ahead for certain tasks. For instance, if you are attending a meeting, won't you prepare for the meeting? Part of that preparation should include reading wide on the topic for discussion, highlighting the key issues and possible solutions to those issues.

There are some people who are great at thinking on their feet at the spur of the moment but not everyone can do that. But being prepared is something everyone can do, and that involves being prepared to sell yourself; the unique value you bring to the team or department you work in, the few minutes you have with the boss, key decision maker, potential client or employer, whether it is in an elevator, a meeting room or elsewhere.

Hack 4

Know your work.
Takeaways:

1. Know your work well and be prepared to talk about what you do.

2. Be present in the moment. Your mind must be actively present on the job daily, paying close attention to the tasks you are given and other relevant information that relates to your work and workplace.

3. Read your tasks, (documents, files and so on) more than once. Statistics reveal that you often forget over 75% of what you have read the first time and retain more, the more times you read something and even much more when you take notes.

4. It helps to keep a note of daily tasks including special assignments and accomplishments, so you can refer to them from time to time.

5. Write down a short profile of yourself and what you do and have a copy on your phone, you never know when it will be useful. Update it with new accomplishments from time to time

When dealing with clients, business partners or any other parties, confidence is essential. People will always look for signs of self-assurance before they truly trust you, which is only natural, because it is difficult to esteem someone who does not esteem him or herself.

Hack 5
Confidence is key.

Ugo was a Banking Officer in a top-tier bank when she was called into the office of the bank Managing Director for a brief one-on-one meeting. She was expecting a difficult conversation and believed he was going to critique the way in which she had handled a recent matter. Much to her surprise though, he wasn't angry. He offered her a seat and then proceeded to give her some excellent advice that has stayed with her ever since.

"It's not just about what you say," he said. "It's about how you say it." He went on to explain that when dealing with clients, business partners or any other parties, confidence is essential. People will always look for signs of self-assurance before they truly trust you, which is only natural because it is difficult to esteem someone who does not esteem him or herself.

He advised her to always use an assertive tone of voice when speaking to others. As he put it, an inept but confident person will always convince others far more easily than a highly competent but unsure person.

"Even if you don't know the answer to a problem, rather than stumbling over your words in embarrassment, it's far more effective to boldly say, 'I'll check on that and get back to you, and then fulfill your word by finding and providing the appropriate information."

Hack 5

Confidence is key.

So ask yourself, in your communications and interactions with others, are you giving off an air of uncertainty and lack of confidence in yourself? Are you fidgeting, shifting in your seat or avoiding eye contact? Or are you speaking clearly and confidently, with your head held high?

The latter approach will always achieve the best results.

However, you can't give what you don't have. You can't display true confidence if you don't possess it internally. To do so, you must refuse to be defined by your past mistakes and failures, because the most important thing is to learn from each one and apply those lessons in order to do better in the future. Identify and recognize your own true strengths, and tell yourself that with determination and diligence, you can achieve whatever you set your mind to. Then, you will find that self-confidence will blossom from within.

Practical steps to display confidence:

1. Dress the part: Never underestimate the importance of how you look. People see what you are wearing before they hear you speak and within a few seconds of meeting you, have decided whether they want to get to know you or not.

2. When you look good you will typically feel good about yourself. When you feel good about yourself those feelings radiate from within and become evident to others.

Hack 5
Confidence is key.

3. A good posture helps you to seem more confident and ultimately become more confident. Merely standing and sitting properly will improve the way you appear and helps you to feel confident and project confidence to others.

4. Speak the part: people who speak clearly and properly are usually perceived as confident and smart. Speaking well doesn't mean you have to speak with an accent but it means you have to know the proper pronunciation of words, be familiar with your industry terminology and use them accordingly.

Something as seemingly trivial as a misplaced semi-colon or comma could case a statement to be interpreted differently from the writer's intention, with costly and far-reaching implications.

Hack 6
Pay attention to details.

There is a common phrase – 'the devil is in the detail' but I will like to state emphatically that success in the work place is in the details.

Abiodun used to think he was a stickler for details until he met a very meticulous boss. His boss always focused on making each and every piece of work not just good, but truly excellent.

Mrs. Zainab was a very thorough reviewer whose sharp eyes would pick up even the smallest errors. She would often ask Abiodun, "Have you checked XYZ?" just to make sure that the pertinent details were accurate in every document. Through working with her, Abiodun learnt the importance of thoroughly checking his work to prevent the sort of small errors that can easily lead to big problems. In fact, Abiodun acquired eagle eyes himself, and always spotted what was missing in most documents. This earned him the role of being the reviewer in a subsequent workplace, amongst his other work duties. Abiodun's attention to detail had become legendary that he became saddled with reviewing his colleagues and supervisors' reports before they were sent to the boss. In fact Abiodun's boss wouldn't review any report unless it had Abiodun's sign off on it.

When it comes to written matters, it is exceptionally important to pay attention to detail. Something as seemingly trivial as a misplaced semi-colon or comma could cause a statement to be interpreted differently from the writer's intention, with costly and far-

Hack 6
Pay attention to details.

reaching implications. This is true of every field of endeavour. Whether it's a lawyer reviewing an agreement or a report to be delivered to a Governor; a carpenter measuring out the exact dimensions of a table; a singer learning the lyrics of a new song, or a CEO examining a company's monthly performance; every successful professional must pay close attention to detail.

So the next time you're given a task, pay close attention to the details, which means closely reviewing the data that goes into the work, as well as the eventual output. Before submitting the final output, go over it with a fine-toothed comb; then go over it again. Where appropriate (for instance, where confidentiality and other requirements permit) you can even ask a trusted and capable friend to lend you a fresh pair of eyes by helping to review the final output.

Take the time to cast a critical eye over the finer points of your work. You'll be glad you did. Your boss will too.

Takeaways:

1. Mistakes make you look unprofessional and unreliable, try as much as humanly possible to avoid them.

2. Engage in peer review, have trusted colleagues look over your work, and do the same for them.

Hack 6
Pay attention to details.

3. Don't have an "*anyhow*" mentality, it will show up in your work. Always seek excellence, it's hard but it pays off in the long run.

Imagine the errors that can be corrected, jobs that can be saved, and misunderstandings that can be averted if only we spoke up. So as scary as it may be to speak up in Naija, you must speak up when it matters.

Hack 7
Know when to speak up.

Abou was friends with the guys in the Accounts Department so he had access to some confidential information about staff salaries. He found out that his colleagues who were on the same level as him were earning more than him. After living with this knowledge for about six months, Abou handed in his resignation letter. At the exit interview, when asked why he was leaving the company, he said it was on account of the fact that his salary scale had not been adjusted in the past year and it had come to his knowledge that his colleagues who were on the same level as him were earning more than him. Management checked with the Human Resources personnel (HR) and Accountant and discovered that it was an oversight. This was a matter that could have been resolved if it was escalated to management as soon as Abou discovered the salary differences, however it was too late for Abou, he had already handed in his resignation letter.

Sheyi shared an experience about the importance of speaking up. She was retained at the firm where she did her mandatory NYSC, but since she was employed as a permanent staff in the middle of the month, she was told her salary would be prorated – calculated to reflect the amount of time she had spent as an employee. Therefore, instead of being paid ₦40,000 which was the monthly salary, since she had worked for only half of the month, she was paid ₦20,000. At the end of the following month, Sheyi noticed that her salary, though higher than the previous one, was not a full month's salary. As soon as she discovered the error, she escalated

Hack 7

Know when to speak up.

it to HR who went with her to discuss with the Accounts department. At Accounts, it was discovered that since there was a note to pro-rate the salary for the previous month when she started work mid-month, the note hadn't been taken off. Accounts rectified the error for both Sheyi and her colleagues who were also affected, and they thanked Sheyi for speaking up.

The Managing Director later sent for Sheyi and informed her that he learnt she was the one who pointed out the error. He thanked her for pointing it out and added that he hoped she paid similar attention to detail with her work as well. Sheyi assured him that she would and she did.

Imagine the errors that can be corrected, jobs that can be saved, and misunderstandings that can be averted if only we spoke up. So as scary as it may be, to speak up in Naija, you must speak up when it matters.

Takeaways:

1. Do not suffer in silence. When you feel you have been passed off on a promotion or are being treated unfairly, speak up and inform Management about it. State your case professionally (without mentioning the names of other colleagues), in a manner that suggests you require clarification and not stated as an accusation.

Hack 7

Know when to speak up.

2. Speak up as soon as possible; it may help to articulate your points well, by writing them down and reviewing them with a trusted advisor or mentor. This will help you put things in context and present the issues clearly.

3. Having a workplace mentor (where possible) will help a great deal in navigating some dark and murky waters of office politics.

4. As much as it is key to know when to speak up, also know when not to speak, be discreet too. Private matters that others share with you about their health and personal dealings at work, for example, should be kept to yourself.

Bode missed out on a very good job and an even better opportunity on account of not being able to take correction from his boss. Don't be like Bode at your workplace. Please keep a tight rein on your emotions. Don't let them rule you.

Hack 8
Rule your emotions.

Bukola was the Managing Director of a multinational and on one occasion she had to caution a member of staff whose actions led to a blunder, which almost cost the company. She called Bode to her office and spoke to him firmly about the potential damage his actions could have cost the company and demanded that he be extremely careful going forward. He apologized and promised it wouldn't happen again. An hour later, he came back to her office with his resignation letter. Bukola was taken aback as she wasn't expecting this at all. The only explanation for Bode's behavior was that he didn't like being reprimanded in any manner whatsoever. The following day, Bode went in to see Bukola and admitted he had let his emotions get the better of him the previous day and he would like to withdraw his resignation. Bukola was shocked to hear this, but informed him that his resignation letter had been sent to the Human Resource department and the process for his exit had already been triggered. It was therefore too late for him to withdraw the resignation.

As bad as that was, that isn't the end of the story. Shortly after Bode's exit from the organisation, another opening came from one of the company's subsidiaries. Bode applied for the position to head the subsidiary and he scaled through the first and second stages of the recruitment process.

After the third and penultimate stage of the interview they needed to make one final call. It was to his previous employer. Bukola received a phone call informing her that Bode had scaled through the interviews and her opinion was required on Bode's suitability

Hack 8
Rule your emotions.

for the leadership position since they had worked quite closely in recent times. She acknowledged that Bode was bright and very skilled, however she stated emphatically that he was highly emotional and didn't take well to being corrected. She also noted that giving Bode the job would seem like he was being rewarded for unprofessional behavior in the parent company and would send a wrong signal to other employees. I must add that the new job came with a much bigger salary and perks. The recruiters agreed with her and Bode didn't get the job.

Bode missed out on a very good job and an even better job opportunity on account of not being able to take correction from his boss. Don't be like Bode at your workplace. Please keep a tight rein on your emotions, don't let them rule you.

Bode obviously did not know the importance of 'practicing the pause' which is, delaying making very important decisions in the heat of the moment, while you're very upset or very happy.

Takeaways:

It helps to consider the following before you take a decision immediately after a work incident that you're not happy about:

1. Take a deep breath and count to hundred. If you're still agitated, count to two hundred. As simple as it sounds, it could

Hack 8

Rule your emotions.

help to ensure you don't say or do something in the heat of the moment.

2. Wait at least twenty-four to forty-eight hours or even a week after, before taking action and see if you still feel the same way about the incident. Chances are you won't feel the same way and if you do, whatever decision you will be making then, will be a well thought out one, not an emotional decision.

3. Take a break from the situation. You'll be amazed at how your perspective will change about a situation, if you take a step back from it. A few casual days off work, with permission of course, could do a world of good.

4. Discuss the work situation with a trusted person first, before taking a decision - this could be a friend, family member, or mentor. It is usually not advisable to discuss the incident with a colleague at work.

What do you do when you develop feelings for someone at work, you may ask? After all, you naturally grow to have affection for people you interact with closely, daily.

HACK 9
Don't piss where you eat.

My Boss said this so many times. If there was ever a hint of colleagues having an affair in the office he would say loudly, "I hope there's nothing going on! You must never piss where you eat." Now let me explain that phrase. As it implies, where you eat is usually a place you want to keep clean and pleasant. If you're like me you won't ever sit near the toilet facilities at a restaurant. Starting a relationship at your workplace is very risky especially when it doesn't end amicably. When the affair is over and you both still have to work together, it typically ends up being uncomfortable for the parties involved and the people who have to work with them. There are exceptions but it often doesn't end well. It's like peeing around where you're eating; it would be smelly and awkward wouldn't it?

Nnamdi started having an affair with his supervisor at work. It was a very secret affair, only one or two people at work knew about it. After a few months, they ended the relationship. Things started getting messy for Nnamdi at work, his supervisor started issuing him queries, sometimes very unnecessary ones, until eventually he was fired. Nnamdi not only lost a relationship, but an upward moving career path and his current source of livelihood.

HACK 9

Don't piss where you eat.

Is it worth risking your career and source of livelihood because of a workplace affair? It usually gets messy. Yes, there are a few happy endings you may say but in those cases one person usually leaves the workplace. In most offices, workplace relationships are discouraged and prohibited on account of it usually affecting the work dynamics of the parties, their colleagues and ultimately their work productivity in the company.

If you won't eat your food in the toilet and go to toilet where you're eating your food, then you shouldn't have work place relationships. When you do that you're pissing where you eat!

What do you do when you develop feelings for someone at work, you may ask? After all, you naturally grow to have affection for people you interact with closely, daily. Truth is, I know of quite a number of people who found love at work and it resulted in marriage. For workplace relationships that worked out, they kept the relationship very private and one of the parties sought and gained alternative employment. In other cases, one of the parties was a Corps member and was only at the organisation for the one-year mandatory youth service.

Takeaways:

1. Read your workplace handbook to know what it says about workplace relationships. It is prohibited in a lot of organisations but acceptable in others.

HACK 9
Don't piss where you eat.

2. If you do entertain a relationship with a colleague keep it away from work, it must be strictly confidential and you must do everything possible to ensure it doesn't interfere with your work and interaction with other colleagues. It is important to remember that in every relationship at work, you should be professional.

3. Consider the consequences in the event the relationship ends and ask yourself whether the person is worth the huge risk of losing your source of income.

4. One party should consider leaving to search for a job elsewhere. If it is a serious relationship both parties would discuss their career prospects and goals before deciding on who makes the move.

5. It is useful to know that in Multinationals, workplace relationships are permitted, but they would typically require that parties disclose to the organisation when a relationship exists or occurs in the course of work, to avoid conflict of interest. In such cases reporting lines must be changed to ensure the parties involved don't report to each other.

When you share knowledge with colleagues and supervisors you become a resource person within your organisation and that can only earn you respect from peers

Hack 10

Be quick to learn, and after you've learnt, teach.

and superiors and ultimately, promotion.

In the Nigerian work environment you will find out that a lot of people will hoard knowledge and information. They feel that's how to stay relevant but as counter intuitive as it may sound, the way to stay ahead is by sharing what you know with others.

Aisha used to run a Non-Governmental Organisation with a staff strength of five permanent staff and over one thousand volunteers. At some point, the Chairman of the Board informed her that a Project Manager had been appointed and would resume work within a month. Aisha was put in touch with the Project Manager immediately and began to educate her on various work processes and projects. A few members of the team were livid and said: *"Listen! How can you be sharing everything with her, don't you know she might be your replacement?"* Aisha's attitude was that even if she was her replacement, the professional thing to do would be to handover and she remembered a popular saying – *'no one is indispensable.'* For Aisha, this meant that no matter what information she hoarded, she wasn't indispensable. Someone else would someday do her job and as the pioneer leader of the organisation it was important to her that she passed on enough information and tools for her successor to succeed, because failing to do so would not only be a slight on her successor but on Aisha too.

Hack 10

Be quick to learn, and after you've learnt, teach.

Even if you are not moving on from an organisation the fact that you have trained someone to fit into your role leaves an avenue for you to be promoted to a higher role both within the organisation and elsewhere. Shortly after the Project Manager resumed and 6 months into her role as Project Manager, it gave Aisha the chance to pursue another opportunity, which was much better and more fulfilling in so many ways.

The fact that Aisha had shared so much information with the new Project Manager, made it easy for her to make a smooth transition, without destabilizing the organisation. Whatever position you find yourself, whether as a new recruit or a seasoned professional, it is important to share knowledge and information. When you share knowledge with colleagues and supervisors you become a resource person within your organisation and that can only earn you respect from peers and superiors and ultimately, promotion. When you share knowledge with subordinates, you instantly communicate to management that you are leadership material and that earns you quick access to managerial roles within the organisation.

Ultimately, when you fail to share what you know and what you've learnt you do more harm to yourself than your workplace. At the workplace it pays more to share than to hoard information.

Takeaways:

Hack 10

Be quick to learn, and after you've learnt, teach.

1. You rise up faster by helping others in the work place. When you teach others and assist them with difficulties on the job you are perceived as a leader and will be given positions of responsibility.

2. When you keep your knowledge to yourself and you don't pass it on to others, you actually end up being stuck in a position for a long time. It stunts your growth instead of accelerating it.

3. Helping people in the workplace is the key to building helpful relationships that would help you both inside the workplace and beyond.

The minute her performance started dwindling and management had to make cutbacks her name was top on the list.

Hack 11 (Bonus)

Past glory doesn't last.

Amaka was a very hardworking and efficient employee. In a word she was a *'performer'* and an asset to her boss. When her boss got a better role in another company, Amaka was one of her first recruits. At first Amaka brought her 'A' game on but a month later she started to come up with one excuse or another to be absent from work. At some point the company had to downsize and it happened during one of her legendary disappearances. Human Resources (HR) recommended her dismissal and the boss promptly agreed. A few days later Amaka sent her boss a tale of woes about how she was going through a rough patch in her relationship and her spouse was making a comeback, hence her disappearances from work. Since she had now sorted things out with her spouse she would like her job back.

Her boss did not respond immediately as she was shocked at Amaka's effrontery to ask for her job back in spite of her recent poor performance. Amaka's boss in her response reminded Amaka that she was employed first, to do a job! Her unavailability to do that job irrespective of why she was unavailable, was the primary reason for her dismissal.

Hidden in her boss's response is another work place hack - your boss's concern is in you getting your job done, you were employed to work! Your boss is not concerned about personal matters that may hinder your work performance so please keep them private. Everyone goes through issues now and again, but as much as you can, you must keep your private matters separate and must not let them interfere with your performance at work.

Hack 11 (Bonus)
Past glory doesn't last.

Amaka was one of the first recruits upon her boss's new role based on her past glowing performance in her previous job with her boss, but her past performance wasn't enough to sustain her at her new job. Amaka needed to bring her 'A' game into her new role and consistently too. The minute her performance started dwindling and management had to make cut backs her name was top on the list. She was dismissed.

You'll keep being assessed based on your performance so you need to be a consistent performer to thrive at the workplace.

Takeaways:

1. Accept that you will have some challenges but determine not to let them affect your productivity at work.

2. You can decide to take some leave from the office, in case your private issues are too overwhelming, and especially when they begin to affect your state of mind and wellbeing.

3. Have a good support system to help you handle the emotional side of life, when life goes awry.

Hack 11 (Bonus)

Past glory doesn't last.

4. Tough times don't last, but tough people do. Determine that no matter how hard it gets, you will keep showing up and doing your work well.

Hack 12 (Bonus)

Keep a trail of certain conversations.

In the world of bosses as with many spheres of life there is the good, the bad, the ugly, and the very ugly. Yes, we are Nigerians, and we are extra in everything. Most bosses will tell you the importance of keeping a proper paper and online trail of all communication with clients. In fact, some will insist that they are always kept in copy in all online correspondences. However, your boss will not tell you to keep a trail of personal communication with him or her. With the boss who turns into a very ugly one this piece of advice is priceless.

Tola worked with a hardworking yet fierce boss, who was fond of giving her subordinates various terms of 'endearment' – well, that's how subordinates were forced to see it. Names such as *lemon, olodo, dodo*, were commonplace in her vocabulary and she pretty much got away with it, until one day Tola had had enough.

After calling her *lemon* for failure to obtain a number from a client, Tola went back to her supervisor's office and politely said

'Ma'am, please I don't respond well to name-calling.'

Her supervisor immediately said "Oh sorry darling, I hear you."

Tola thought that was the end of the matter only to receive this text message from her:

Hack 12 (Bonus)

Keep a trail of certain conversations.

"Darling, I don't know why you and other ladies here are too sensitive, when I say the same thing to the guys they're cool about it and get on with the work. Please stop getting so emotional and grow some balls!"

Tola's response:

"Ok ma'am if growing some balls means I can give you an appropriate response next time you call me *lemon* I will take this text as permission to do so."

Her supervisor's response:

"Well, you better hope I'm not wearing my knuckle duster that day, otherwise it will land in your face..."

Tola didn't have any further response to that and shared the text exchange with a colleague at work.

Hack 12 (Bonus)

Keep a trail of certain conversations.

As time went by, Tola's supervisor stopped assigning tasks to her, but Tola didn't bother as she was getting assigned work from other senior staff. When it was time for annual appraisals, Tola's supervisor refused to appraise her work. An appraisal was critical to receiving an annual bonus, so Tola didn't receive an annual bonus and eventually decided to move on. During her exit interview, when asked why her supervisor didn't appraise her, she said she knew it was personal and shared what had transpired between herself and her supervisor. All Tola could do was talk, but at that time it was too late, especially as she had no evidence to back her assertions! She had not saved those phone messages. Although they were phone messages she ought to have backed them up so that at the appropriate time she would escalate the matter to HR with the messages to back up her claim of being bullied and disrespected by her supervisor.

When Tola's supervisor was informed of Tola's resignation she called her on the phone and said:

"Tola the intention was to get your attention, not for you to resign."

Tola, in shock, said "Ma'am you had my attention all the while."

Some months later, Tola received a phone call from her former supervisor saying she was sorry about the whole incident and she hoped Tola had no hard feelings towards her.

Hack 12 (Bonus)

Keep a trail of certain conversations.

For the two of them, it ended amicably but it could have had a different conclusion if the matter was handled professionally.

Some conversations with superiors, be it in the form of text messages and emails, should be properly archived so they can be recalled when required.

What Tola faced at work was a form of bullying and if that happens to you or is happening to you, please don't suffer in silence. Matters like these should be reported to your HR/Personnel manager with evidence to back your claim. With most phones these days you can archive your messages. Emails can also be backed up in the cloud. It is easy to keep a trail of written documents and it is also helpful to have a personal file of some documents you may need to refer to later.

My boss didn't share this with me and no boss will share this with you, but it is probably one of the most valuable hacks for saving yourself in the workplace against a very ugly boss.

Takeaways:

1. Keep track of communication in the workplace, including informal communication, in instances where you feel

Hack 12 (Bonus)
Keep a trail of certain conversations.

threatened and uncomfortable. This applies to bullying and other forms of harassment.

2. Don't entertain any form of bullying, disrespect or harassment. Escalate to Human Resources as soon as possible. You must bear in mind that in some organisations even after escalating the situation, you may still have to leave the organisation but it is likely you will be in a position of strength, if you have evidence to back your claims.

3. Some workplaces can be toxic. In the event you find yourself in a toxic environment, start looking for the way out. Hardly does anyone grow in a toxic environment.

4. Note that this hack is not encouraging you to record all conversations at work. In fact, it's best practice to seek permission before recording conversations with another person, in order to avoid breaking certain privacy laws.

5. This hack is for situations where you feel threatened and should be used in those exceptional circumstances with a very ugly boss.

Conclusion

I added the last two bonus workplace hacks because while hacks 1-10 will help you proactively keep your job. Hacks 11 and 12 are vital to ensure that you do not by your action or inaction contribute to your own dismissal! Hack 12 is particularly important to ensure that when you face a very ugly boss, you have armed yourself with your own defence, and as far-fetched as it may sound, it is a true-life story.

This book was born out of the feedback received in comments and direct messages (DMs) on what I tagged 'Workplace Wednesdays' which I shared on a weekly basis through short videos on my Instagram page @thetemitopegeorge. People would *slide into my DM* and ask questions like "Did that really happen? Do things like this really happen in Naija?" Others would say "I really want you to share my experience too but you must tell it in a way that it can't be traced to me nor my workplace" and I assured them I would. The interest from those snippets propelled me to document them in this book. I hope you will learn from them and in turn share some of your personal experiences with me so that others can learn from them too.

In the words of Maya Angelou "When you learn, teach. When you get, give." These Hacks are my way of doing just that.

Please feel free to reach out to me on Instagram @thetemitopegeorge, follow, like, comment, send a message and learn from the free tips I offer for work place efficiency.

ABOUT THE AUTHOR

Temitope George is a British Trained Barrister (of Gray's Inn) and a Legal Practitioner of the Supreme Court of Nigeria with over 16 years experience up to managerial levels in the private and public sector.

She has spoken on workplace readiness, professional etiquette, and executive presence on numerous platforms some of which are:

- LEAP Africa School to Work Programme
- Facilitator with Fifth Gear Consulting graduate marketplace readiness programme with the NYSC
- Nigerian Law School.
- Various tertiary institutions.
- Corporate Bodies
- Social Enterprises; and
- Government Agencies

She also featured on CNN's Inside Africa sharing insights on the impact of Social Media on Nigerian Youths and Entrepreneurs.

Her hobbies include vlogging where she shares Etiquette Tips on her YouTube channel (EtiquetteTipsWithTG) and her Instagram page @thetemitopegeorge, where she shares tips on workplace efficiency, executive presence and professional etiquette.